ROOMS IN A BURNING HOUSE

A Mind-Mansion in Three Acts

by K.W. Krieger

Copyright © 2024 K.W.Krieger

All rights reserved. This book, or parts thereof,

may not be reproduced in any form without permission.

Independently published

Cover art Copyright © 2024 K.W.Krieger

ISBN: 978-1-7644967-4-2 (Paperback)

ISBN: 978-1-7644967-5-9 (Hardcover)

This is a work of fiction. The events described here are imaginary: The names, settings, places, and characters are fictitious and not intended to represent specific places or persons, living or dead. Any resemblance to actual events or persons is entirely coincidental.

Dedication

For everyone who has lived in a house of their own mind
and believed they were alone in its rooms.

For those who walk through darkness with quiet bravery.
For those who carry invisible weights with trembling hands.
For those who survived their own fire.

This book is for you.
May you find echoes here — not of pain alone,
but of the truth that you are understood,
and you are not walking these halls by yourself.

For the Reader

This book moves through rooms shaped by mental illness, memory, and survival.
Some may feel familiar. Some may feel heavy. Some may open without warning.

You are allowed to read slowly.
You are allowed to pause.
You are allowed to leave rooms that feel unsafe today.

Nothing in these pages asks you to relive what hurt you.
They are here only to witness what already exists.

The doors do not close behind you.
The house will wait.

Trigger Warning

This book contains poetic depictions of:

- Anxiety, panic, and fear
- Depression and suicidal ideation (implied, not graphic)
- Trauma, PTSD, and childhood emotional neglect
- Psychosis, hallucinations, and delusional thinking
- Eating disorders, body dysmorphia, and starvation themes
- Addiction and substance withdrawal
- Self-harm tendencies (metaphorical references)
- Dissociation, depersonalization, and identity fragmentation
- Mania and emotional dysregulation
- Disorders involving compulsions, tics, and intrusive thoughts.
- Grief, loss, and overwhelming emotional states

While these portrayals are artistic and symbolic,
they may be triggering to some readers.

If you feel distressed while reading:
Pause. Breathe. Reach out to someone you trust.
Your mental and emotional safety comes first.

If you are in crisis or struggling with suicidal thoughts,
please seek help through your local emergency number
or a mental health crisis hotline in your area.

You are not alone.

Author's Note

This book is not a diagnostic tool,
nor is it meant to define anyone's lived experience.

Each poem is a metaphorical room,
a symbolic representation of the emotional landscape
that mental health disorders can shape our surroundings.
No two experiences are alike,
and nothing in these pages should be taken
as a universal description of any condition.

These pieces were written
to honor the complexity,
the pain,
the resilience,
and the humanity
of those who navigate mental illness.

If you see yourself in these rooms,
I hope you feel witnessed.
If you see someone you love,
I hope you understand them a little more.
If you see unfamiliar rooms,
I hope they widen your compassion.

Most importantly:
If you are struggling,
please know help exists —
and you deserve to reach for it.

Table of Contents

INTRODUCTION
- Welcome to the Burning House
- Interlude I: *At the Threshold*

ACT I — THE LIVING HOUSE
- Interlude II: *Where the Architecture Breathes*

The Foyer — Anxiety

The Dining Hall — Binge Eating Disorder

The Observatory — Bipolar

The Basement — PTSD

The Library — OCD

The Master Bedroom — Major Depression

The Attic — Schizophrenia

The Study — ADHD

The Hall of Mirrors — Borderline Personality Disorder

The Ballroom — Dissociation

The Nursery — Childhood Trauma

The Cellar — Addiction

The Gallery — Social Anxiety

The Clocktower — Insomnia

The Conservatory — Panic Disorder

The Winter Garden — Seasonal Affective Disorder

ACT II — THE HIDDEN WINGS

- Interlude III: *Rooms That Should Not Exist*

The Infinite Corridor — Agoraphobia

The Surveillance Room — Paranoia

The Weaving Room — Trichotillomania

The Accumulating Room — Hoarding Disorder

The Hall of False Windows — Delusional Disorder

The Paralysis Chamber — Sleep Paralysis

The Infirmary of Echoed Symptoms — Somatic Symptom Disorder

The Collection Chamber — Kleptomania

The Hall of Mirrors Reborn — Narcissistic Personality Disorder

ACT III — THE ASH-WALK

- Interlude IV: *Walking Through Ash*

The Bedroom Ruins — Bereavement Disorder

The Library Ruins — Rumination

The Ballroom Ruins — Catatonia

The Attic Ruins — Amnesia

The Summer Garden — Autism

The Shattered Conservatory — Tourette's Disorder

The Broken Clocktower — Fatigue Disorder

The Empty Gallery — Avoidant Personality Disorder

The Split Nursery — Dissociative Identity Disorder

The Empty Cellar — Substance Withdrawal

The Scorched Study — Gender Dysphoria

The Collapsed Foyer — Hypervigilance

The Ash Kitchen — Restrictive Eating Disorder

The Furnace — Mania

THE EXIT

- **Interlude V:** *The Door at the End of the House*

Final Poem — What I Carry Out of the Fire

ACT I — THE LIVING HOUSE

Welcome to the Burning House

This book is a house.
It stands tall in the mind, with doors that lock themselves and corridors that shift when no one is looking. Some rooms glow warmly, lined with memories soft as blankets. Others burn quietly behind their walls, smoke seeping through floorboards in thin, familiar breaths.

This house is not meant to frighten you, though parts of it may.
It is meant to show the places where many of us live, whether by choice, by chance, or by the fragile wiring of our own brains.

Each room in this mansion represents an experience —
a disorder, a symptom, a memory, a wound, and a way of surviving.
Not clinical definitions, but felt realities.
Not stereotypes, but echoes of real human storms.

The rooms shift.
They multiply.
Some disappear until you return to them years later and discover they were always there, waiting.

This is what navigating mental illness can feel like:
a life lived inside architecture that rearranges itself around you.

In the first part of this book, the mansion is alive.
We walk through its halls as it grows, flickers, expands, rearranges — a mind illuminated from within, sometimes too brightly, sometimes not at all.

In the second part, we move into the deeper wings:
the hidden chambers, the impossible staircases, the places the
light doesn't reach until the house reveals them.

And in the final part, we return after the fire.
Walls charred.
Floors collapsed.
Rooms exposed for what they really were once the smoke
clears.

This is not a book about being "broken."
It is a book about the architecture of feeling —
about what it means to carry many rooms inside you,
some safe, some dangerous, all of them yours.

If you enter this house, do so gently.
Some rooms may resemble places you've lived.
Some may remind you of people you know.
Some may open without warning.

But you are not alone here.
You walk with a guide —
with language,
with imagery,
with compassion for every corner of the mind.

Welcome.
Take the key.
The house is listening.

INTERLUDE I

At the Threshold

The door stands taller than memory.
Its brass handle is warm,
as if someone has just let go.

Behind me, the world I came from waits
in its ordinary colors.

Ahead, the mansion inhales.

A single ember glows
beneath the floorboards.

I step inside.

The door closes
without touching it.

INTERLUDE II

Where the Architecture Breathes

The corridors shift with every footstep,
stretching, tightening, opening like lungs.

Walls pulse with quiet life.
Portraits watch with patient eyes.

The house seems to learn me
as I walk it.

Every room that opens
feels like a truth I wasn't ready to remember
but have always known.

The Foyer — Anxiety

Footsteps in the Foyer

The house greets me
with its thousand ticking throats—
clocks, pipes,
a settling of beams
that feel like bones deciding
whether to break.

Every sound becomes
a possible someone.
Every shadow
tries on the shape
of danger.

My hands want the doorknob
even after I've shut the door.
My mind keeps checking
its pockets
for a thought it must have dropped—
a warning,
a whisper,
a thing I forgot that might
undo everything.

I cross the floorboards
like a guilty secret.
Their groans accuse me.

My breath rehearses
excuses I haven't earned.
My pulse stalks me
down the hallway
like a footstep
half a second behind.

A house this large
shouldn't feel so
close.

A body this small
shouldn't be asked
to hold so many alarms.

But here I am—
the foyer flickering
as if something
just out of sight
has exhaled.

And I,
unable to stop listening
for the next sound
that says
run.

The Dining Hall — Binge Eating Disorder

The Endless Table

The table is long,
and I sit at its far end,
a solitary guest
at a feast
I never meant to host.

Plates gather
like unasked questions—
warm, fragrant,
waiting for the moment
my resolve thins
like cooling steam.

I reach for one
before I decide to—
hand moving faster
than thought,
as if the hunger
borrowed my body
to answer itself.

Flavors bloom,
rich and immediate,
softening the edges
of a day
that cut too sharply.

I eat to quiet,
to steady,
to soften,
to make the world
a little less loud.

One plate becomes two,
then a constellation
of small disappearances—
each bite a hush,

a pause,
a brief forgetting.

Fullness rises
before comfort does.
But still I reach,
chasing the place
where satisfaction
was supposed to live.

The chandelier watches,
its light trembling
as if unsure
whether to bless
or condemn.

I shrink beneath its glow—
not smaller in body,
but smaller in worth,
folding inward
as the table expands
with my wanting.

When I finally stop,
the silence returns
too quickly,
too sharply—
a cold draft
through a broken window.

I sit among the remnants,
the plates half-pushed away,
the air thick
with the sweetness
that never stayed long enough
to soothe what ached.

The hunger
was never in my stomach.

It lived deeper—
a hollow behind the heart,
a quiet room
no food can fill.

And now,
as my body settles heavily
into the chair,
the table waits.

It has learned my patterns.
It knows
I will come back
not because I desire more,
but because I desire
less hurt
than before.

The Observatory — Bipolar

Skyfire in the Observatory

Tonight, the stars
recognize me.

They lean in,
tilting their bright skulls
as if to say,
finally, you're awake.

Telescopes bloom
like metal flowers,
their glass throats
drinking starlight
and offering it to me
unfiltered.

Constellations rearrange
themselves
to spell my name—
or I read it there,
which feels the same.

My thoughts outpace
the turning of the heavens.
Galaxies spin
like coins I've tossed
into a wishing well
with no bottom.

If I climb high enough,
I could thread a comet
through my ribs
and call it
purpose.

If I speak loudly enough,
the moon would answer
with her white, wide smile

and we would share secrets
that crackle like kindling.

The dome's brass ribs hum.
The universe inhales.
I swear I can feel the house
beneath me
warming,
catching,
glowing—
as if my pulse
has become a fuse.

I am incandescent.
I am limitless.
I am a lantern
left too close to the drapes.

The Basement — PTSD

The Basement with No Switch

The stairs creak
in the same pattern
every time.
My body knows it
before my mind does.

Down here,
the dark hums
like a bruise remembering
how it happened.

I keep one hand
against the wall—
its cold breath,
It's rough insistence
that the past
has architecture.

Something rattles.
A pipe.
A chain.
A memory unwinding itself
in metal syllables.

I tell myself
nothing is down here.
I tell myself
it was years ago.
I tell myself
the house is empty.

But the dark
has a good memory.
It calls me
by the old name
I don't use anymore.

Shadows lean long
across the floor,
touching my ankles—
not grabbing,
but close enough
that the old fear
shakes awake,
stretching its jaws.

I breathe too fast.
I listen too hard.
I wait for the thing
that isn't here
but still lives
in my blood.

There is no switch.
There is only
returning.
There is only
the sound of something
behind me
that isn't real
but used to be.

I climb the stairs
two at a time,
as if outrunning
memory were possible—
as if it didn't already have
a room reserved
in the basement
and a spare key
to my sleep.

The Library — Obsessive–Compulsive Disorder

Catalogue of Certainties

The books must stand in perfect, even rows.
I touch each spine to feel its quiet proof.
Order is the only truth I know.
Disaster waits beneath a single roof.

I touch each spine to feel its quiet proof—
four taps, then two, then one to seal the spell.
Disaster waits beneath a single roof;
I check the latch to make sure all is well.

Four taps, then two, then one to seal the spell.
The lamp must glow at just the proper height.
I check the latch to make sure all is well—
the wrongness in the room would spark the night.

The lamp must glow at just the proper height;
I count the seconds—six—and then again.
The wrongness in the room would spark the night
unless I pace the pattern I maintain.

I count the seconds—six—and then again.
Order is the only truth I know.
Unless I pace the pattern I maintain,
the books won't stand in perfect, even rows.

The Master Bedroom — Major Depression

The Bed That Keeps Its Dead

The drapes hang heavy with a sullen grace,
their velvet shoulders sagging under dust.
The mirror turns its pale, unblinking face
away from mine, as if it has no trust.

The sheets remember shapes I used to make—
a curled confession, drawn in creases deep.
The bedside clock performs its small heartbreak,
ticking an elegy to hours I keep.

I move so little, even ghosts grow bored;
they drift toward brighter rooms with easier air.
My body feels a kingdom overthrown—ignored,
its bannermen dismissed for lack of care.

This bed, a tarnished throne I can't ascend,
crowns me in stillness I cannot defend.

The Attic — Schizophrenia

Voices in the Eaves

The attic bends
where the roof remembers
lightning.

Shadows gather
in the rafters—
not malign,
just watching,
as if waiting for me
to finish a sentence
I don't recall starting.

A radio hums
though it has no cord.
It speaks in languages
I almost understand—
half-words that bloom
into warnings,
or welcomes,
or both.

The dust moves
like something breathing.
A trunk creaks open
without asking me.
Inside:
photographs of people
I've never met
but who know me
too well.

One says my name.
Not aloud—
but the way a mirror
says your face.

The house tilts
like a thought unraveling.
The rafters whisper,
not unkindly:

We have always been here.
We have always been here.

I blink,
and their silence
finishes the sentence
for them.

The floorboards pulse.
The air thickens.
Somewhere below,
the house keeps burning—
but up here
the fire has already learned
to speak.

The Study — ADHD

The Desk with Half a Thousand Beginnings

The book is open
to a page I meant to read—
or was it the next one?
The margin doodles bloom
like restless vines
doing anything
but staying still.

A pen rolls off the desk,
and suddenly I'm under it,
finding last week's notebook,
a receipt,
a bright idea I scribbled down
that still feels brilliant—
until I stand up
and forget it.

Sunlight catches the dust—
tiny galaxies—
and I remember
I once planned to learn astronomy.
I spin the chair.
The chair spins me.
Momentum counts as progress, right?

A timer goes off
for something
I no longer recall starting.

The book is still open.
The room is still spinning.
My thoughts are a flock of starlings
bursting in twelve directions—
no leader,
no landing place,
just the beauty
of motion.

If I could catch one,
just one,
the whole study might make sense.
But another flashes by—
shinier—
and I follow,
forgetting
what I meant to begin
when I first sat down
at this desk
with half a thousand
beginnings.

Hall of Mirrors — Borderline Personality Disorder

The Mirror Teaches Me My Faces

Every mirror in this hallway
wears a different version of me.

In the first, I am loved—
glowing, untouchable,
a candle someone has cupped carefully
so the wind won't win.

In the second,
I am already leaving,
though I don't remember why.
The frame trembles
from the door I must have slammed
before I even opened it.

The third mirror whispers
that I am everything:
radiant, rare,
a brilliant burn of wanting.
I press my palm against the glass
to feel it back.
It doesn't.

The fourth says
I am nothing.
Its silence is a verdict
I swallow too quickly.

Further down,
the reflections multiply—
me adoring,
me destroying,
me abandoned,
me abandoning—
a gallery of selves
that take turns
holding the blade.

At the last mirror
I ask,
"Which one is real?"

It cracks
down the middle,
dividing the question
into two truths
I cannot carry at once.

And in the splintered glass
I see
every version of me
reaching
for the same impossible
steady
face.

Ballroom — Dissociation

"The Dancer With No Shadow"

The ballroom glows
with chandeliers that fall
from nowhere.

Music pours in
but no musicians stand
to claim it.

I step onto the marble—
light as a thought
I can't quite catch.
My feet touch the floor
like someone else's memory.

I lift my hands.
They hover,
obedient,
weightless—
the gestures of a puppet
I am watching
from another room.

Couples drift around me,
faces blurred,
edges shimmering
like paint thinned with too much solvent.
Their laughter echoes
through a corridor
I cannot walk down.

I dance—
or rather,
I witness the body
that wears my name
turn beneath a chandelier
that refuses to cast
its shadow.

The music slows.
My pulse stays still.
I blink,
and the room becomes
a watercolor trembling with water—
everything soft,
everything melting.

When the lights dim,
I look for myself
among the silhouettes
pressing toward the exits.

But I find only
the shape of a woman
I do not feel
living behind my ribs,
spinning slowly,
slowly,
slowly,
like a lantern
that has forgotten
its flame.

The Nursery — Childhood Trauma

The Room That Keeps Its Cradles

The wallpaper still holds
its pale parade
of moons and rabbits,
faded from the years
I don't remember
but my bones do.

A rocking chair
sways gently
with no one in it—
a lullaby
with no mother
to finish the tune.

The crib remains,
small as a held breath,
its bars painted white
so no one would notice
the places I learned
to grip silence.

Stuffed animals watch
from their shelves,
stitched smiles steady,
button eyes knowing
more than they should.

Here,
the air tastes
like the seconds
before someone shouts,
like the stillness
that teaches a child
how not to be seen.

I kneel on the rug—
stars in soft blues and gold—

and touch the place
where the carpet
is slightly darker,
where a spilled secret
soaked in
years ago.

Nothing moves.
But the room hums
with a story
I have told no one:
the smallness,
the waiting,
the quiet footfall
of fear learning my name
before I ever
spoke it.

When I stand,
the rocking chair stops
as if the room itself
has finally
exhaled.

The Cellar — Addiction

Barrels, Bottles, Promises

The cellar smells
like old wood
and older lies.

A bare bulb swings,
casting its slow halo
over barrels
that once held wine
and now hold
something heavier.

Bottles line the shelves
like soldiers
waiting for command—
clear glass throats
ready
to swallow
whatever part of me
I offer.

I descend the steps
the way a needle
finds a vein—
automatic,
familiar,
graveled with guilt.

The walls sweat.
My hands shake.
The bulb flickers,
a warning
I pretend not to see.

I tell myself
just tonight.
I told myself that
last night,

and the one before
that made
the one before
collapse
quietly.

The bottle opens
with a sigh
that sounds like forgiveness.
Or permission.
Or surrender.

The first swallow burns.
The second warms.
The third—
I don't remember.

At the bottom of the stairs,
the light sways,
tired of watching me
circle the same drain.

Upstairs, the mansion burns.
Down here,
I pour another
and call it
water.

The Gallery — Social Anxiety

Portraits With Eyes That Follow

In the gallery,
every frame tilts slightly
toward me—
a silent choreography
of suspicion.

Faces painted centuries ago
seem to whisper
behind their varnish.
Their brushstrokes stiffen
when I pass.

I tug my sleeves
into safer lengths.
My breath becomes
a rehearsed performance
I cannot perfect.

Footsteps echo
far too loudly—
mine,
but wearing the weight
of a hundred judgments.

A couple at the far wall
glances up.
I become
a trembling exhibit—
"Figure With Nowhere to Look."

My throat knots.
My tongue hides.
Small talk curdles
before it reaches my teeth.

The room narrows
into a corridor
of glances.

I wish to be invisible,
but invisibility
is an art I never mastered.

Instead, I stare
at a portrait of a girl
with downcast eyes—
her avoidance framed
in gold.

We understand each other.
We both stand very still
and try not to be seen
any more
than we already are.

The Clocktower — Insomnia

The Hours Refuse to Sleep

The gears grind
with delicate cruelty,
turning time into
a sleepless theology.

Midnight rings—
a cold, clean sound—
and I lie beneath it,
wide-eyed as the moon.

The clocktower breathes
in metallic sighs,
exhaling seconds
like sparks.

I count them.
I lose count.
I start again.

The mattress curls
like a question mark
I can't resolve.
Sheets tangle—
restless serpents
coiling around my hope
for rest.

At 2 a.m.,
time sticks its tongue out—
drags each minute
like a dull blade
across my nerves.

At 3 a.m.,
the gears whisper stories
I never agreed to hear.
Regret is a pendulum

swinging inches
from my ear.

By 4 a.m.,
the shadows soften,
tired of themselves.
Even the dark
begins to yawn.

But the moment
I close my eyes—
the tower strikes again,
and the day begins
without asking
if I ever ended
the night.

The Conservatory — Panic Disorder

Glass Room With Breaking Heartbeats

A single breath
splinters
in the glass-walled room.

Plants tremble
in pots too still
to explain the trembling.

Light fractures
into sharp white shards—
I can't tell if it's the sun
or my pulse
doing the cracking.

Air thins
like someone wrung it
from the room.

My ribs tighten—
a fist closing
around a fist.

I try to speak
but the sentence collapses
into gravel.

Something enormous
and unseen
presses its weight
onto my chest.

My vision narrows
to a tunnel
with no promise
at the end.

The conservatory
tilts—

glass panes expanding
and shrinking
with each frantic beat.

My heart behaves
like an animal
snared,
thrashing
for escape.

The plants blur.
The floor breathes.
My hands spark with static
I cannot shake away.

Then—
as suddenly as it came—
the pressure cracks,
splinters,
dissolves.

The room still stands.
I still stand.
But every leaf trembles
with the memory
of breaking.

The Winter Garden — Seasonal Affective Disorder

The Garden That Forgot Its Sun

The garden sleeps
too deeply this winter.
Snow crowds the air
with pale exhaustion.

Branches sag—
shoulders weighted
by the absence
of color.

Even the statues
seem colder,
their stone eyelids
half lowered
in resignation.

I walk the frostbitten path
with careful steps,
each footprint filling
with silence.

The sun rises late,
a tired coin
pressed into a sky
that has forgotten brightness.

Flowers dream
under frozen earth—
dreams sluggish,
muted,
barely warm enough
to keep living.

I feel myself
mirroring them—
a seed refusing
to split open,

a stem curling inward,
a color drained
by months of gray.

The winter garden
does not ask me
to bloom.
It simply waits,
aching with me,
for the light
to remember
our names.

ACT II — THE HIDDEN WINGS
INTERLUDE III

Rooms That Should Not Exist

Past the grand staircase,
the floor tilts slightly—
a suggestion that gravity is negotiable.

Doors appear
where wallpaper once was.
Staircases spiral into rooms
that echo themselves.

Here, the mansion forgets
that it was ever a house.

Here, the mind invents
its own blueprints.

What waits behind these doors
is not always illness,
but the shape illness leaves.

The Infinite Corridor — Agoraphobia

The Hallway That Opens Into Too Much

The corridor stretches
farther than architecture allows—
a long, pale throat
swallowing distance.

Every door stands open,
inviting,
empty,
endless.

The more space I see,
the less room I feel
inside my own breath.

Walls pull away
from each other
like they are tired
of holding me up.

The ceiling rises,
slowly,
until it is no longer a ceiling
but a blank sky—
featureless,
infinite,
indifferent.

My footsteps scatter
in every direction
at once.
I cannot tell
which echo belongs to me.

Air yawns wide.
My pulse shrinks.
Space expands
until my own body

feels like the smallest corner
in existence.

I try to move forward—
but every step
dissolves beneath me,
becoming another yard
of unbearable sky.

I turn back.
The hallway behind me
is also infinite.

This is a trap
made of open space—
a maze whose walls
have all fallen outward.

The freedom
is the danger.

The exit
is everywhere
and nowhere
at the same time.

The Surveillance Room — Paranoia

The Room With Too Many Keyholes

There are eyes
in the wallpaper.
Tiny ones—
inked into the floral swirls
like concealed seeds.

The ceiling hums
with a quiet electricity
that knows my name.

Cameras bloom
from the corners—
black pupils
set in mechanical petals.

Every shadow
leans forward
to hear me breathe.

A dozen doors
line the circular wall.
Each has
a keyhole,
a peephole,
a listening hole
drilled at just the height
where secrets travel.

Behind one of them,
someone inhales.
Behind another,
a whispered syllable
breaks like a twig.

I hold my breath.
The room holds it with me.

A red-light blinks—
once,
twice,
as if taking note.

The floorboards shift
under my feet,
rearranging themselves
to follow my weight.

I check behind me.
Nothing.
But the nothing
moves
when I move.

This room
collects me
bit by bit—
a dossier of footsteps,
a catalog of glances,
a file of fears.

Someone is watching.
Something is watching.
Or perhaps
the watching
is inside me—
a creature with mirrored eyes
that never blink
at the same time.

The Weaving Room — Trichotillomania

Threads Pulled From the Self

Looms fill the room,
each one threaded
with strands of hair—
long, short,
dark, pale,
recognizable.

Mine.

I sit before the nearest frame
and feel the familiar itch—
a tug beneath the scalp,
a question asked
by the roots of me.

My fingers answer
before thought can intervene.
A single strand slips free—
a soft surrender,
a tiny release.

The loom accepts it
with the patience
of a confessor.

I weave.
Over, under,
pull, release.
The patterns are imperfect,
but the ritual is perfect.
A quiet ache
made useful.

Behind me,
the room expands—
loom after loom,
cloth after cloth,

a gallery of woven
small violences.

I tell myself
it's just one more strand.
But the loom knows
how many times
I've said that.

Each tapestry on the walls
shimmers slightly—
a self-portrait
made of compulsion,
memory,
and relief.

When I rise,
the room rustles.
The woven hair
sways gently
as if breathing.

As if living.

As if waiting
for me to return
and finish
what I never meant
to begin.

The Accumulating Room — Hoarding Disorder

The Room That Grows Around Me

It starts small—
a stack of newspapers
rising like sediment
from a forgotten decade.

Then a box,
then another,
then ten,
filling the corners
with soft avalanches
of once-needed things.

The room expands
to make space
for what I cannot release.

Books pile into towers.
Clothes spill
in fabric tides.
Old letters drift
like brittle snow.

The more I place down,
the less the room resists.
It stretches,
accepts,
invites.

Every object whispers
its reason to stay—
You might need me.
You once loved me.
You can't throw away
what remembers you.

The door narrows.
The air thickens.

I carve thin pathways
through mountains
of meaning.

Each step
requires negotiation
with history.

Each corner
asks for mercy.

The ceiling lowers
under the weight
of all the things
I could not choose
between.

I tell myself
I'll sort it tomorrow.
But the room grows
while I sleep,
stacking,
sprawling,
protecting me
from the empty space
that terrifies me
more than clutter
ever could.

By morning,
there is only a narrow slit of light
and the gentle pressure
of a room
trying to keep
everything
from slipping away.

Including me.

The Hall of False Windows — Delusional Disorder

The Windows That Show What Isn't There

Each window in this hallway
opens to a world
that insists on being real.

Through the first:
a city where every passerby
wears my face—
different clothes,
different ages,
but unmistakably me.

Through the second:
a forest glows
with bioluminescent script,
trees spelling out messages
in a language
that disentangles itself
as I watch.

Through the third:
a stranger sits in a room
identical to mine
and mouths my thoughts
a moment
before I think them.

As I move forward,
the windows brighten,
eager to be believed.

Landscapes bloom
with truths
no one else can see.
People wave
from impossible distances.
A distant figure points
directly at me

from a horizon
that curves unnaturally inward.

I reach for a latch—
but the glass is warm
as skin.

Behind me,
the hallway rearranges itself,
windows shifting like eyes
tracking a single
vital revelation:

Everything here is a message.
Everything means something.
Everything connects.

And though part of me hesitates,
the rest of me leans closer,
ready to believe
whatever world
opens next.

The Paralysis Chamber — Sleep Paralysis

The Bed Where Shadows Sit

The room darkens
before my eyes open.

Something presses
onto my chest—
not weight,
but a presence
shaped like inevitability.

I try to move.
My limbs remain
marble,
cold,
unwilling.

The ceiling crouches closer,
its corners warping
into silhouettes
that drip
downward.

A figure sits
on the edge of the bed.
Featureless.
Expectant.

It leans near enough
that I feel its breath
though it has no mouth.

My heartbeat hammers
against the ribcage cage
that will not unlock.

The air thickens—
not choking,
but claiming.

A whisper threads itself
through the dark:
a language I have never heard
but somehow recognize
from the oldest parts
of fear.

I scream internally.
The scream goes nowhere.

The shadow moves
only when I don't watch it.
Only when the dark
fully remembers me.

When my body finally jolts
back into motion,
the room is empty.

But the shape of that presence
remains etched
into the silence—
a warning,
a residue,
a recurring dream
that hunts
in waking light.

The Infirmary of Echoed Symptoms — Somatic Symptom Disorder

The Examination That Never Ends

In the infirmary,
every surface gleams
with sterile certainty.

A clipboard floats
beside the exam table—
pages flipping
in a breeze
that has no source.

My body lies before me
like a riddle
I've been solving
for years.

The stethoscope listens
too closely.
Each beat
magnified
into a small catastrophe.

A flicker in my chest
becomes
a tremor in the lights.
A pinch in my side
ripples through the floor,
tiles shifting
as if bracing for collapse.

The instruments hum
with eager diagnosis.
Thermometers glow.
Pressure cuffs tighten
without hands.

Every ache I name
blooms into existence—

a bruise of blue light
across the wall,
a phantom pain
etched into the air.

A doctor appears,
faceless,
cloaked in white noise.
She asks where it hurts.

I point everywhere.

She nods
as if this too
is a symptom.

As I sit up,
the room bends
with me—
validating sensations
I cannot disprove.

In the infirmary,
my body becomes
a story
that keeps writing itself
whether or not
I want to hear
the ending.

The Collection Chamber — Kleptomania

The Things That Call to Be Taken

The chamber glitters
with objects
small enough to pocket—
coins,
pins,
charms,
keys to doors
I'll never open.

Each one hums
with soft invitation.

I tell myself
I don't need them.
But need
is not the point.

It's the thrill
of touching something
no one expects
to be touched.
The hush
before the taking.
The moment
before ownership
changes hands.

My fingers twitch—
a magnetic pull
toward things
that sparkle
with forbidden simplicity.

A silver thimble
rolls toward me
as if asking
to be chosen.

A locket cracks open
on its own—
its empty interior
glimmering
with possibility.

The room rearranges,
setting small treasures
along my path,
each one lit
with a quiet plea:

Take me.
Nobody will notice.
I belong to you now.

When I slip a stolen trinket
into my pocket,
the chamber sighs—
a soft, approving exhale.

The object warms,
claiming me
as much as I claim it.

And though shame lingers,
it is gentle—
eclipsed
by the comfort of possession
I never meant
to desire.

The Hall of Mirrors Reborn — Narcissistic Personality Disorder

The Mirror That Kneels

In this hall,
the mirrors rise
taller than memory,
stretching upward
like cathedral glass.

But unlike cathedrals,
they worship
me.

My reflection stands
in perfect poise—
chin lifted,
eyes bright
with borrowed divinity.

When I move,
the mirrors lean closer—
adoring witnesses
to brilliance
I am certain
I possess.

They whisper compliments
with silvered tongues:
You are exceptional.
You are singular.
You are more.

I bask
in the glow
of my multiplied selves.

But as I walk deeper,
the reflections lag
by half a second—
a delay

too slight to deny,
too sharp to ignore.

One mirror shows me
taller.
Another shows me
sharper.
Another shows me
hollow
around the eyes.

Still, they bow.

Still, they praise.

Still, they insist
I should remain here,
centered
in endless admiration.

When I reach for the nearest glass,
my reflection clasps my hand
with hunger—
a grip too tight,
a need too deep.

I pull back.
It does not.

In the shimmering tension
between us,
I realize:

The mirrors do kneel—
but only because
they cannot stand
without me.

And I cannot stand
without them.

ACT III — THE ASH-WALK
INTERLUDE IV

Walking Into the Memory of a House

The stairs no longer creak.
There is nothing left for them to say.

Ash lies in soft drifts
where carpets once carried warmth.
The windows are bare frames—
skeletons of light.

Each room I enter
feels smaller than I remember,
as if the flames have shrunk
what once felt infinite.

I walk slowly.
Not because I fear what I'll find,
but because the silence
is a fragile animal
and I do not wish to disturb it.

The mansion no longer shifts.
It only waits.

I breathe in
the faint, acrid memory of fire,
and begin the final journey.

*The Bedroom Ruins — Complicated Grief /
Bereavement Disorder*

The Bedframe That Still Holds an Impression

The fire spared this room
in the cruelest way.

The mattress is gone,
burned to a soft black outline,
but the bedframe remains—
charcoal ribs
holding the memory
of a body
that once warmed it.

Dust outlines
where a picture frame stood.
The photograph is ash now,
but the rectangular absence
is so precise
it could still be a face.

A single shoe survived
beneath the window.
Its partner vanished
into smoke
months ago.
I cannot throw it away.

Everywhere I look,
there is evidence
of someone who isn't here.

An indent in the wall
where laughter once leaned.
A crack in the floor
where arguments gathered.
A shadow
that refuses to leave
the corner.

Grief, I've learned,
is not the fire.
It is the ember
that outlives it—
the small, stubborn glow
that refuses
to go dark.

Even now,
the bedframe waits
for a weight
that will never return.

I touch the ash
where a hand once rested,
and feel it warm
beneath my fingers.

The Library Ruins — Rumination

Ashes Repeating Themselves

The library is dust now—
shelves collapsed
into gray dunes,
books reduced
to brittle murmurs.

Yet somehow,
the words survive.

I step across the charred floorboards
and ash rises
like phrases
trying to rebuild themselves.

A burned page lifts—
collapses—
lifts—
collapses—
as if caught
in a draft of thought
that cannot stop
revising itself.

Every corner whispers
the same question
in softened consonants:
what if what if what if what if—

I try to walk past it.
But rumination
is a gravity
stronger than flame.

The ash rearranges
into patterns
I can almost read:

a fear,
a memory,
a doubt,
a scenario
that never happened
but feels truer
than the truth.

The shelves breathe
with repetitive intent.

The burned books
remain open
to the same page
no matter which one
I reach for.

I brush off the ash.
It settles back
into the same sentence.

In this room,
nothing stays destroyed.
The thoughts
rebuild themselves
endlessly
from the ruins.

The Ballroom Ruins — Catatonia

The Dance That Never Resumes

The chandelier fell
and froze
in a crown of fractured glass.

The fire didn't melt it.
It simply
halted it—
caught mid-collapse
like a gesture
interrupted.

The dance floor is dusted
with cinders and glitter—
indistinguishable now.

Chairs sit overturned
in patient disarray.
They seem to wait
for movement
that will not return.

I stand in the center
of the vast, ruined room
and realize—

I cannot move either.

Not forward.
Not back.

A stillness
settles over me
like soot.

The air hangs heavy
with unspent motion,
as if the fire paused

right before
touching the heartwood.

In catatonia,
there is no fear,
no desire,
no urgency—
only the absence
of the ability
to begin.

The mansion quiets
around me,
mirroring my stillness.

Even the dust
refuses
to fall.

The Attic Ruins — Amnesia / Memory Loss

The Room With Missing Corners

The attic is open now—
half its roof gone,
sky spilling in
where secrets once gathered.

Boxes sit melted
into soft, collapsed shapes.
Labels are burned off.
I do not know
what any of them held.

Photographs lie scattered
across the floor,
their faces erased
by smoke—
all outlines,
no features.

I pick up a picture.
I know
it should hurt
that I can't recognize
who stood beside me.

But the fire
burned away the pain
along with the names.

Memory loss
is a gentle thief.

The attic rafters
are broken,
yet harmless.
Nothing leaps out.
Nothing shouts.

Nothing reminds me
of what I've forgotten.

A faint warmth
lingers in the beams
as if the fire
tried to tell me something
before it died.

I look at the boxes
with no labels
and feel only
a quiet curiosity:

Who was I
before the flames
rewrote me?

The attic doesn't answer.
It simply holds the sky
where the roof used to be.

The Summer Garden — Autism

The Garden Too Bright to Enter

The snow is gone.
Summer has claimed everything.

Where once the garden slept,
the colors now scream—
sunflowers blazing like open mouths,
roses bleeding red
onto the cracked pathways.

The light is too loud.
The heat presses hard
against my skin
in textures I cannot ignore.

Every petal vibrates
with unbearable detail.
Every bee hums
in a frequency
that enters bone.

People say the garden is beautiful now.
I nod,
but the brightness claws
at the edges of my senses.

I walk carefully,
mapping the safe stones,
cataloguing the shade,
counting breaths
until the world softens.

In the center,
the fountain lies toppled—
water spilling gently,
rhythmically,
predictably.

I sit beside it
and let the repetition
quiet the colors
one hue at a time.

I am not broken here.
The world is simply too large
all at once.
And I am learning
which corners of it
will let me breathe.

The Shattered Conservatory — Tourette's Disorder

Glass That Jerks in Its Frame

The conservatory is cracked now—
panels trembling
in uneven rhythms
no wind caused.

Shards twitch on the floor,
jumping slightly,
clicking together
like teeth.

My body mirrors the room—
movements firing
before meaning,
before choice.

A shoulder jerks.
A sound escapes—
sharp, involuntary,
a syllable made of spark.

The glass replies
with its own small spasms,
as if echoing
my uncontrollable pulse.

Vines crawl through the broken wall,
their tendrils twitching
in little spasms
that feel too familiar.

I try to still myself.
Stillness refuses me.

A hand snaps forward—
a gesture without intent.
A word bursts—
a note without song.

The shattered panes
sing back with their own
irregular chorus.

Here in the broken conservatory,
I see that the world, too,
jerks sometimes—
cracks,
stutters,
releases sound
it never meant to make.

And maybe
I belong here
more than anywhere else.

The Broken Clocktower — Fatigue Disorder

The Clock That Forgot to Move

The gears have melted
into soft, slumped shapes—
no more grinding,
no more relentless rhythm.

The tower stands hollow,
too tired
to measure anything.

Time has pooled
on the floor
like spilled oil—
thick, unmoving.

I try to lift the pendulum.
It drops
from my fingers.
I do not try again.

Even the dust
settles slowly here,
falling asleep
before it reaches the ground.

My body feels the same—
too tired to break,
too tired to heal,
caught in the dull gravity
of endless depletion.

Where once the hours
tormented me
with their metallic tyranny,
now they lie slack
and silent.

Burnout is not fire.
It is ash
falling inward.

The clock does not tick.
Neither do I.

We rest together
in this room
that has forgotten
how to wake.

The Empty Gallery — Avoidant Personality Disorder

The Walls Where Pictures Should Hang

The gallery is bare now—
frames removed,
nail-holes staring
like tiny regrets.

No portraits watch me.
No crowd's whisper.
The silence is a relief
and an indictment.

I walk along the walls
and imagine
what might have hung here—
faces I avoided,
rooms I left too early,
affections I stepped around
like broken glass.

There are labels
beneath each blank space,
but the words
have peeled away.

I stop in front
of the largest wall.
A plaque reads:
"Untitled: The People Who Would Have Stayed."

I cannot look at it long.

Avoidance is not absence—
it is a presence
too large to face.

The gallery gives me
the gift of emptiness,
the luxury of space

where judgment
cannot bloom.

And yet...

Every blank wall
leans toward me,
asking softly:

*What might have lived here
if you had stayed?*

The Split Nursery — Dissociative Identity Disorder

The Cradle in Two Places at Once

The nursery has divided.

A seam runs through it—
not quite physical,
not entirely imagined—
a split in the air
where the room forks
into two realities.

On the left side,
the rocking chair
moves gently,
comfort in its rhythm.

On the right,
it sits still,
too still,
as if listening
to something unsaid.

Toys shift
from one side to the other
when I blink.
A stuffed bear sits
in both halves at once,
its expressions mismatched—
gentle here,
guarded there.

Voices hum
from two corners—
not echoes,
but companions,
each carrying a version
of the same memory
told in different light.

I feel myself
split with the room—
one foot in each world,
each grounded
in a different truth.

The nursery
does not ask me
to choose a side.
It simply holds
every version of me
that needed
to survive.

The Empty Cellar — Substance Withdrawal

The Cellar That Trembles

The bottles are gone.
But their absence
is loud.

The walls shiver
with a cold
that lives beneath the skin.
The bulb flickers—
not from weakness,
but from memory.

My hands shake.
The floor shakes with them.
The whole cellar
seems to rattle loose
from its foundations.

Sweat beads
on the stone walls
like the room itself
is detoxing.

I breathe hard.
The air bites—
metallic,
merciless.

The body remembers
what it wants.
It remembers
what it fears.

Withdrawal is a double-edged thirst—
one blade for the substance,
the other for the self
I barely recognize.

Something in the dark
whispers promises
I know are lies.

Something in the light
offers suffering
I know is truth.

I grip the railing,
ride the tremors,
and wait for my blood
to stop burning.

Upstairs,
the mansion is quiet.

Down here,
the cellar shakes
until the shaking
becomes the only proof
that I'm still alive.

The Scorched Study — Gender Dysphoria

The Desk With the Wrong Name Carved Into It

The study burned hottest here.

The desk is warped,
It's engraved initials
half-melted—
belonging to someone
I was told
I should be.

The mirror
hangs cracked on the wall,
reflecting a face
in jagged fragments—
None of them
quite mine.

Books on the shelves
have titles scorched off.
Identity manuals
turned to ash.
Pronouns erased
by smoke.

A coat hangs from a hook:
the wrong cut,
the wrong weight,
a costume
I never chose.

I sift through ashes
until I find
a piece of the mirror
small enough
to hold.

When I lift it,
my reflection bends—

not distorted,
not wrong,
just unfinished.

The fire
did not destroy me.
It burned away
the versions
I was never meant to wear.

In the scorched study,
I see myself—
not clearly,
but honestly.

And that
is more than I ever had
before the flames.

The Collapsed Foyer — Hypervigilance

The Doorway Still Listening

The foyer has caved in—
roof fallen,
door hanging by a hinge
that no longer catches.

The alarms are gone.
But the silence
is sharpened.

Every creak of settling ash
twitches along my nerves.
Every shifting shadow
reminds my body
how to brace.

I know there is no danger here.
But knowing
is not the same
as believing.

Hypervigilance lives
in the hollows
left by fear—
a ghost instinct
that refuses
to move on.

The door hangs open,
harmless now.
Yet I watch it
as if it might slam
without warning.

The foyer waits
for a threat
that isn't coming.

So, do I.

The Ash Kitchen — Restrictive Eating Disorder

The Cupboards That Echo

The kitchen is hollow.
Cupboards gape open—
emptied by fire
or by me,
I can't tell which.

Plates lie cracked
on the blackened counter.
Silverware warped
into thin, fragile lines.

A bowl sits untouched
in the center of the floor—
a lonely moon
in a dark sky.

The refrigerator door
hangs open,
light still flickering
weakly inside.
Its shelves are bare.

My stomach twists—
not with hunger,
but with the absence
of hunger.

I run my fingers
along the cold counter,
feeling the sharpness
of nothing.

This room
once held feasts
I denied myself.

Now it holds
only ash.

The fire burned
what I refused to take.
Between us,
we starved the kitchen
to silence.

I stand in the doorway
and feel my ribs ache
with old mathematics—
calories,
penance,
control.

But the kitchen
offers nothing now.

And maybe
that emptiness
is a beginning.

The Furnace — Mania

The Heartfire That Wouldn't Go Out

The furnace still glows,
even though the rest of the mansion
has surrendered to ash.

Coals throb with leftover brilliance—
not flames,
but memory of flames,
pulsing like a heartbeat
that never learned moderation.

The walls surrounding it
have melted inward,
glass pooled like captured lightning
at my feet.

I can almost hear
what the fire once said—
a language of sparks,
rapid, ecstatic,
relentless.

In Act I,
this room thundered with purpose—
every ember an idea,
every flame a certainty.

Now the fire flickers
with uneven breath,
as if exhausted
by its own brightness.

I kneel before it.

Heat licks my skin
with the tenderness
of something dangerous
that remembers being worshipped.

Mania is a sun
that rises too quickly
and sets in ruin.

Yet here—
in this wreckage—
the furnace still glows.

Not to consume.
Not to dazzle.
But simply
to exist.

A quiet, trembling ember—
the last remnant
of a brilliance
that nearly burned me whole.

I stand.
The ember dims,
but does not die.

It will follow me out
as warmth,
not wildfire.

THE EXIT

INTERLUDE V

The Door at the End of the House

The walls thin
as I approach the final room—
so thin
I can hear the world outside
breathing.

The mansion has stopped shifting.
It no longer rearranges itself
to reflect my fears,
my compulsions,
my fractures.

It simply waits.

In the quiet,
I realize:

I have walked through
every room
I once feared to name.

I have held
what was burning.
I have stood
in the ruins.
I have learned
the shapes my mind can take
when the storm is inside.

The final doorway
stands open—
charred at the edges,
but open.

Beyond it,
I see morning.

Not salvation.
Not certainty.
Just morning.

I step toward it.

The mansion exhales,
releasing me
from its long-held breath.

I place my hand
on the scarred doorframe,
not to steady myself—
but to say goodbye.

Final Poem — Upon Exiting the Mansion

What I Carry Out of the Fire

When I leave the mansion,
the smoke parts around me
like a curtain
granting passage.

The morning air is cool—
a mercy
after rooms that swallowed heat,
after hallways
that stretched too wide,
after attics that whispered
and cellars that begged.

I turn once
to look back.

The house stands
in its wounded glory—
burned,
broken,
but still a house.

Inside it
are all the versions of me
I once was:

the trembling one
pressing her ear to the foyer door,
the frantic one
chasing her own heartbeat
through the conservatory,
the starving one
sweeping empty plates
into empty cupboards,
the luminous one
painting galaxies
on the observatory walls.

None of them disappear
when I step outside.

They walk with me—
not as weights,
but as witnesses.

The world beyond the mansion
is not easier.
But it is wider.

And I am wider too—
made of corridors
that taught me to navigate darkness,
rooms that held
what I could not name,
fires that illuminated
what I thought was ruin
but turned out
to be understanding.

I hold the key in my pocket.
I do not need it,
but I keep it—
a reminder
that the mind is a place
I can return to
on my own terms.

As I step into the day,
I carry no flames.
Only embers—
small, warm,
enough to light a path
but never again
to consume me.

And this,
after all the rooms,

all the smoke,
all the mirrors—
is enough.

Final Thoughts

If you've reached this page,
you've walked through every room of the burning house
and stepped into the quiet that follows.
That is no small thing.
It is a testament to your willingness
to witness what is difficult—
both within these pages
and perhaps within yourself.

The mind is a mansion
far larger than the rooms we show others.
Some doors open easily.
Some hallways echo.
Some attics whisper in the dark.
Some basements remember more
than we wish they did.

And yet, even in its darkest wings,
the mind is capable of rebuilding—
of reshaping structure from ash,
of finding new footing
in the smoke that once obscured everything.

Nothing here claims to capture
every experience of mental illness.
No single house could hold
the infinite shape of human pain
or the resilience that rises beside it.

But I hope these rooms
offered a moment of recognition,

or compassion,
or quiet understanding—
whether for yourself
or for someone you love.

If you saw your own shadows here,
may you feel a little less alone.
If you saw someone else's,
may you carry this knowledge with gentleness.
And if you found only unfamiliar corridors,
may they still expand your capacity
to see the unseen rooms in others.

We are houses always being remade.
We are wanderers learning
that fire does not always mean destruction—
sometimes it reveals,
sometimes it transforms,
sometimes it clears the foundation
for something truer to rise.

Thank you for stepping inside.
The journey does not end here.
it continues in every act of understanding,
every moment of softness you allow yourself,
every time you recognise
that you do not walk alone
through the rooms of your own mind.

From my house to yours,

K.W. Krieger

Rest here awhile.

www.ingramcontent.com/pod-product-compliance
Lightning Source LLC
Chambersburg PA
CBHW070945080526
44587CB00015B/2224